THE STORY OF BRITAIN: IN THE MIDDLE AGES

The author's lively approach to history and the artist's brilliant illustrations in both colour and black and white brings the past vividly to life in *The Story of Britain*, which was originally published as one volume.

The author, R. J. Unstead, is renowned as 'the young reader's historian'. He wrote his first book, *Looking at History*, when he was the headmaster of a school in Hertfordshire.

The artist, Victor Ambrus, has illustrated many books for children and has been awarded the Kate Greenaway Medal of the Library Association.

3 cde

Also available in this series

THE STORY OF BRITAIN: BEFORE THE NORMAN
CONQUEST

THE STORY OF BRITAIN: IN TUDOR AND
STUART TIMES

THE STORY OF BRITAIN:
FROM WILLIAM OF ORANGE TO WORLD WAR II

THE STORY OF BRITAIN:
IN THE MIDDLE AGES

R. J. UNSTEAD

THE STORY OF BRITAIN: IN THE MIDDLE AGES

Illustrated by Victor Ambrus
Carousel Editor: Anne Wood

TRANSWORLD PUBLISHERS LTD
A National General Company

THE STORY OF BRITAIN:
IN THE MIDDLE AGES

A CAROUSEL BOOK 0 552 54002 1

Originally published in Great Britain by
Adam and Charles Black Ltd.

PRINTING HISTORY
Adam and Charles Black edition (one volume entitled
The Story of Britain, which forms the Carousel edition
of *The Story of Britain: In the Middle Ages* and the
companion Carousel volumes *The Story of Britain: Before
the Norman Conquest, In Tudor and Stuart Times* and *From
William of Orange to World War II*) published 1969

Carousel edition published 1971
Carousel edition reprinted 1971
Carousel edition reprinted 1972

Carousel Books are published by Transworld
Publishers Ltd.,
Cavendish House, 57–59 Uxbridge Road,
Ealing, London, W.5

Made and printed in Great Britain by
Cox & Wyman Ltd., London, Reading and Fakenham

**NOTE: The Australian price appearing on the
back cover is the recommended retail price.**

CONTENTS

WILLIAM THE CONQUEROR

THE Battle of Hastings may have been a lucky victory but Duke William had the genius to take advantage of his good fortune. Leaving orders for an abbey to be built where the battle was fought, he marched along the coast and captured Dover. This gave him a strong base close to the Continent from which he moved inland to Canterbury. Then, making no attempt to capture London, he crossed the Thames at Wallingford and pitched his camp at Berkhamsted in Hertfordshire.

There, twenty-six miles from the capital and in command of the routes from the west and the north, the Conqueror waited for the English nobles to come to him. Meanwhile, with practised skill, the Norman horsemen laid waste the countryside.

On hearing news of the disaster at Hastings, the Witan had chosen Edgar the Atheling, Edmund Ironside's grandson, to succeed their fallen king. But Edgar was only a lad, and when the northern earls showed no sign of fight, there was no other leader to raise an army against the Norman invaders.

Deeming it hopeless to resist an enemy who had already beaten Harold and the best fighting-men in England, the Witan sent the Archbishop of Canterbury and young Edgar to offer the throne to the Norman Duke.

On Christmas Day 1066, William entered the Confessor's church at Westminster. Presently, the congregation was heard to accept the new monarch with a loud shout. But the Norman soldiers on duty outside the church, mistaking this noise for the sound of revolt, set fire to the neighbouring houses and began to massacre the inhabitants.

After this violent beginning, the new reign proceeded quietly. Englishmen had known foreign kings before this, and when William declared that he was their lawful king, they accepted him, not gladly, but in the hope that he would prove to be another Canute.

At first there were few changes. William certainly rewarded the chief of his followers with the lands of those who had fought against him but he would not allow the Normans to strip the country bare. Surrounded by a hostile population, the newcomers had to obey the man who had led them to victory.

All seemed so quiet that, by March 1067, William felt able to leave the kingdom to attend to matters in Normandy. No sooner was his back turned than the Norman knights began to help themselves to what they thought were the proper fruits of conquest.

They taxed and robbed the English with such brutal greed that, by the time William returned in the autumn, the country was seething with revolt.

Rebellions broke out in several districts but there was no plan and no accepted leader, and William was able to crush the risings one after another with the ferocity of a man who meant to keep the land that he had won.

All of southern England was mastered when Harold's sons were defeated in the west. Then a more serious revolt broke out in the north, where the men of Northumbria acclaimed Edgar the Atheling who was also supported by Malcolm Canmore of Scotland and by a Danish fleet that sailed into the Humber.

When he had crushed this rebellion, William laid a dire punishment upon the north. He sent his horsemen across the land until there was not a house standing nor a human being left alive. In Durham and most of Yorkshire, the cattle were slaughtered and even the ploughs and farm tools were smashed, so that if any survivors crept back to their blackened acres, they would find no means to till the soil. Those who escaped the massacre fled into Scotland where many sold themselves into slavery. For years great stretches of northern England remained an almost uninhabited waste land.

The last of the English rebels took refuge in the swamp-surrounded Isle of Ely. Here, a thegn named Hereward the Wake, so called from his skill and watchfulness, was joined by Edwin and Morcar, the northern earls, who realized, too late, their folly in not supporting Harold. Under Hereward's leadership, the fugitives defied the Normans until the relentless king built a road across the fens and took Ely by storm. As for Hereward, men said William pardoned his heroic foe and gave him command of an army in France where he died in battle or by the hand of a jealous Norman.

It was a grim-faced king who returned to his capital after the harrying of the north and the capture of Ely. He had tried mildness but now he would rule by fear. Any act of disobedience, any move that suggested rebellion was punished with gruesome cruelty and the

English were steadily removed from their lands. By the end of the reign, nine-tenths of England had passed into the hands of Norman lords.

Meanwhile, in many a town or on some nearby hillock, sullen peasants were made to pile up earth into a mound that was crowned by a tower or keep. Each castle, manned by its Norman garrison, was part of William's plan to overawe the towns and to hold down a nation with a few thousand well-armed troops.

The man who laid his iron grip on England was born to rule. He was eight years old when his father, Duke Robert, failed to return from a crusade and the boy grew up in a turbulent land where his friends were murdered and he had to fight long and bitterly to master the treacherous nobles.

He succeeded because he was brave and cunning. His thickset body was as strong as a bull's, and his spirit was unyielding. The Normans came to know that he had a better brain and more resolute will than any of them and, if they did not love him, they feared and obeyed him like a pack of half-savage hounds.

So cruel that he once had the citizens of a rebel town

flayed alive and their skins hung on the walls for mocking his descent from a tanner, William had a kindlier side to his character. He loved his wife and his troublesome sons; his closest friend was Lanfranc, the pious prior whom he made Archbishop of Canterbury, and, as a devout Christian, he wished to bring peace and justice to the people he ruled.

The Norman barons, however, cared nothing for the conquered English and they grumbled bitterly about the King's refusal to let them treat their vassals as they pleased. Ten years after the Conquest, William had to deal with a major revolt by his barons and, in the fighting, he was actually wounded by his own son, Robert. Yet, when the rising was crushed, the King who could be so merciless gave a pardon to his disloyal son.

In these struggles Englishmen found themselves on the Conqueror's side. He might be a hard ruler, but they knew they could look only to him for protection against the barons and their arrogant henchmen. They did not rebel again even when, for the Domesday Book inquiry, his agents measured every rood of land and counted every pig in order that their value should be known to the last penny. And at his death, the chronicler who sighed so bitterly about the Conqueror's greed, also wrote:

'King William was a man of great wisdom and power ... though stern beyond measure, he was kind to those good men who loved God and we must not forget the good order he kept in the land.'

WILLIAM RUFUS

THE Conqueror died in Normandy in 1087. At the end,
unafraid of death and pain, his mind was filled with
thoughts of his difficult sons and his two kingdoms:

'I have killed thousands of those fine people in England,' he murmured to a priest, 'and many have died of
hunger or the sword. May God forgive me.'

He made gifts to the Church and the poor. Then he
divided his possessions. Robert should have Normandy;
Henry, the youngest son, was to have £5,000 in gold
(which he weighed to make sure he was not cheated),
but to William Rufus, 'the Red', his second son, he gave
the crown of England.

Weakly, he tried to remove his great ring so that
Rufus should take it as proof of his will to Archbishop
Lanfranc. Rufus tore the ring from his father's hand and
left him to die, while he hurried to England to claim the
throne before his brother Robert.

Robert, known as Curthose or 'Short legs', was a
jovial little scoundrel, as brave as a bull-mastiff. He had
no idea how to govern a kingdom and the barons much
preferred the thought of him as their ruler to his tough,
bad-tempered brother.

But Rufus was more than a match for the barons. He
put down a rebellion and banished their leader, Bishop
Odo, to Normandy.

The new king had much of his father's ability but
none of the Conqueror's honesty or respect for the
Church. He made no effort to appoint an Archbishop of
Canterbury when Lanfranc died, but used the Arch-

bishop's income for his own purposes and kept the monks of Canterbury on very short rations.

However, in 1093 Rufus fell ill and, believing himself about to die, repented of his greed. He summoned Anselm, the saintly Abbot of Bec, to his bedside and informed him that he was to be Archbishop of Canterbury. Soon afterwards, Rufus recovered from his illness and began to regret the loss of the Canterbury gold, all the more because the gentle Archbishop refused to be bullied by a blasphemous King. The quarrels between them grew so fierce that Anselm was driven into exile and while he was still abroad Rufus was mysteriously slain.

He was hunting in the New Forest when the party became split up and, according to some reports, the King was alone with a nobleman named Sir Walter Tirel. Suddenly a stag ran out and Tirel's arrow, missing the animal, struck the King who died immediately.

The mystery was never solved. If it was not an accident, it was murder, arranged perhaps by the King's brother Henry or, possibly, by believers in a strange form of witchcraft. At all events, Rufus was dead and, for all his wickedness, Englishmen remembered 'the good peace he kept in the land'.

The Conqueror's third son, Henry, was one of the hunting-party, and as soon as he learned of his brother's death he galloped to Winchester to secure the royal treasury. Three days later, he was crowned in Westminster Abbey, and there was good reason for such unusual haste. Robert Curthose, the eldest brother, was expected home any day from a crusade.

When, therefore, Duke Robert arrived to claim the crown, it was already in Henry's keeping and he had taken steps to win over the English people.

Announcing that he would put an end to 'the evil

customs' of his brother's reign, Henry had arrested Ranulf Flambard, the hated tax-collector, and had recalled Anselm from exile. Some of the barons took up arms in support of Duke Robert, but with the English on his side, Henry had no difficulty in defeating them.

HENRY I, 'THE LION OF JUSTICE'

HENRY I was 'thick-set and strongly made, of moderate height and inclining to fatness, but his black hair falling over his brow and the soft expression of his eyes were a contrast to the fierce look of Rufus'.

In fact, he was as violent, cruel and mean as his brothers, but, because he was a far better ruler, he earned the name of 'Lion of Justice'.

Englishmen looked on Henry as one of themselves since his marriage to Matilda, daughter of Queen Margaret of Scotland, a princess descended from their own great Alfred, and they willingly fought in his army when he invaded Normandy in 1106. At Tinchebrai, they took revenge for Hastings when they stood against the Norman knights and cut them down in droves. Duke Robert was captured and Henry, showing no mercy to his brother, kept him a prisoner for nearly thirty years, until his death in Cardiff Castle.

Master of England and Normandy, as he had always meant to be, Henry ruled harshly. He loved gold and he saw that it came into his treasury and not into the pockets of lesser men. His treasurer, chamberlain, chancellor, stewards and constables were made to work as hard as their master, though he paid them little and left no room for private gain. The sheriffs who collected the taxes came to the King himself and on the black and white squares of a great chequer-board placed counters that stood for gold. Thus, when few could understand written sums, the totals were plain for all to see.

So tight-fisted was the King that he knew the pay, the

number of loaves, the measures of wine and the candle-ends allowed to every royal official. No man was allowed more than two meals a day at the royal table and the King himself lived very plainly, although, by custom, a measure of wine was poured out every evening in case he should need it during the night. Since he never drank it, the servants used to drink it themselves until a night came when he asked for his wine. The trembling chamberlain confessed what had happened and, for once, the stern King relented. 'Do you really receive no more than one measure?' he asked. 'That is very little for the two of us. In future, you must get two measures from the butler, one for you and one for me!'

The barons stood in awe of this masterful ruler and the people had justice. 'No man durst misdo another,' wrote the chronicler of his reign; 'he made peace for man and beast.'

But Henry I had one great anxiety. His Queen had given him only two children: a daughter, Matilda, who was sent to Germany to marry the Emperor Henry V, and a son, William, on whom all the King's hopes were fixed.

Prince William was seventeen when his father took him on a short visit to Normandy. The time came to return and the King sailed in his own ship, giving his son permission to make the voyage in a fine new vessel called the *White Ship*. After feasting ashore with his friends, the Prince came aboard in high spirits and ordered the captain to give the sailors three barrels of wine to drink his health. There was much merry-making and delay, so that it was dusk before the vessel put to sea.

Noble ladies and knights crowded the deck; the sailors, warmed by drink, went carelessly about their tasks and the tipsy helmsman sang lustily as he steered out of the harbour. Suddenly, with a shuddering crash

that threw the passengers over, the *White Ship* struck a
rock and began to sink rapidly. In the darkness and con-
fusion, the captain thrust Prince William into the only
small boat and ordered the sailors to row him to safety.
They had left the stricken ship when the Prince remembered that his half-sister was still aboard and he seemed
to hear her voice amid the screams and prayers.

'Put back!' he cried. 'I must save my sister!'

The sailors obeyed but so many terrified passengers
tried to crowd into the tiny boat that it capsized and the
Prince was drowned.

At dawn, some fisherman picked up a man almost
dead from cold but still clinging to the topmast of the
White Ship. He was Berthold of Rouen, the sole survivor
of the company that had put to sea so gaily on the pre-
vious evening.

For three days no one dared tell the King what had
happened. When at last a page-boy was made to stam-
mer out the story, Henry sat transfixed with horror. Presently, rising as if to withdraw to a private room, he fell

senseless to the ground. Later, he recovered consciousness but, in his grief, he never spoke of his son or the *White Ship*. Indeed, men said that he never smiled again.

Five years later, hearing that the Emperor Henry V had died, Henry sent word to his daughter to join him in Normandy. When Matilda arrived from the Low Countries, the King rose eagerly to greet her. She was now twenty-three, a red-haired beauty with the proud bearing of an empress and the masterful expression of the Conqueror's grand-daughter. The King's heart leapt:

'Daughter,' he cried, as he embraced her, 'I have lost a son but, by God's mercy, I have found him again in you!'

He laid his plans and, at Christmas, the barons and churchmen were summoned to meet the King who told them curtly that they were required to swear an oath to accept Matilda as heir to the throne of England and Normandy. The lords of the realm were horrified. It was an unheard of thing for a woman to rule England and the notion of paying homage to this red-haired girl was an insult to their manhood. But none dared voice his thoughts. They feared Henry and they swore the oath.

Next, Henry looked for a second husband for his fiery-tempered daughter and his choice fell upon Geoffrey of Anjou, called the 'Handsome' and also 'Plantagenet' from his habit of wearing in his helmet a sprig of broom – *planta genista* in Latin. Again, the barons were furious, for the counts of Anjou were their ancient foes, and it went sore against the grain to bow the knee to this good-looking princeling.

However, Henry cared nothing for his nobles' discontent. The succession seemed to be safe when Matilda's marriage produced two fine sons, the elder named Henry in his honour, and in 1135 the King went cheerfully across the Channel to visit them. Shortly afterwards, when he was out hunting, Henry was taken ill and died almost immediately. According to his wishes and the barons' oath, Matilda was now Queen of England.

KING STEPHEN AND THE
EMPRESS MATILDA

HENRY I died on December 1st, 1135, but Matilda
made no haste to claim her kingdom, for she and her
husband Geoffrey had decided to make sure of Normandy before proceeding to England. This delay gave
Stephen of Blois his chance to take the crown.

Son of the Conqueror's daughter, Adela, Stephen had
been Henry I's favourite nephew. He was liked by the
barons and he had spent many years in England where
his marriage to a lady descended from the Saxon kings
had made him popular with the common people,
especially the Londoners.

Thus, although Stephen had taken the oath to
support Matilda, he was given a warm welcome in
the capital where, at Christmas, he was crowned by the

Archbishop of Canterbury. In Normandy, too, the barons accepted Stephen as their Duke in preference to Geoffrey, the hated Angevin.

Charming, brave and generous, Stephen was a failure as a king. Men liked him but they did not respect his rash generosity nor fear his lenient temper. He was described as 'a mild man and soft and good, and did no justice', so that the kingdom, released from Henry I's grip, quickly fell into disorder. In a short space of time, Stephen managed to quarrel with the Church and with many of the leading barons. By 1139, Matilda's opportunity had come.

Leaving her husband to conquer Normandy, the Empress crossed to England and made her headquarters in the west country where her half-brother, Earl Robert of Gloucester, was extremely powerful.

Stephen might have captured Matilda at Arundel soon after she landed, but he chivalrously let her escape, saying that he did not make war on a woman. However, both sides took up arms and civil war broke out in which the rival armies sacked towns and devasted parts of the countryside.

Some of the barons took the opportunity to build illegal castles and to enrich themselves by making private war upon their neighbours until, in some districts, the lords who should have upheld justice were living like robber-chieftains. It was said that if strangers were seen approaching a town, the inhabitants fled in terror and 'men said openly that Christ and his saints slept'.

In 1141, at Lincoln, where he fought so furiously that he broke his sword and axe, Stephen was captured and taken in chains to Gloucester where Matilda had him thrown into a dungeon. As 'Lady of England and Normandy', she rode in triumph to London.

So far Matilda had shown courage and ability, but in

the moment of victory her arrogance lost her the crown. She had been an Empress. She had known the grandeur and flattery of foreign courts and she saw no reason to tread warily in a small island where she had been basely betrayed. So she lost no time in putting the barons and churchmen in their places and when the leading citizens of London came to ask her to respect their laws and liberties, she flared up in anger:

'Come you here to prate of liberties to Matilda the Empress?' she stormed. 'Get you back to your counting-houses and talk no more of liberties!'

But when she laid a tax on the city, the Londoners rose against her like a swarm of angry bees until, deserted by all except Earl Robert and a few friends, she was obliged to leave the capital.

Stephen's heroic Queen pursued her with an army and besieged her so closely at Winchester that she and Earl Robert decided to break out at night. In the darkness, they lost touch with each other, and although Matilda rode through the night and came safely to Gloucester, the Earl was ambushed at a ford and captured.

Without her most faithful supporter, Matilda's cause was hopeless and she had to agree to release Stephen in exchange for Robert. The war broke out again but Matilda's cause grew weaker and weaker. She sent Robert to Normandy to beg for help from her husband, but in his absence she was hotly besieged at Oxford where Stephen surrounded the castle.

It was winter and her position became desperate. Earl Robert had not obtained sufficient troops to make an attack across the snow-covered country, and inside the castle the famished garrison was exhausted. But Matilda, as fiery as ever, had no intention of surrendering. One night she had herself and three knights lowered by ropes from the castle walls. Dressed in white garments, they passed unnoticed across the snowy fields and reached the Thames. The frozen river served as a road to lead them to an abbey where they obtained horses and rode to Wallingford Castle.

Here, Matilda was overjoyed to find not only Earl Robert but her nine-year-old son, Henry, who stoutly declared that he had come from Normandy to fight for his mother.

But her chance had gone. She carried on the struggle for five more years until Robert, her valiant half-brother, died. In despair, the Empress retired to Normandy, but she refused to give up her hopes:

'Never forget that one day you will be King of England,' she would say to her son after he had recited his lessons.

By the age of fifteen, Prince Henry was already a dashing warrior. After two adventurous attempts to renew the war in England, he went off to fight in France and presently he married Eleanor of Aquitaine, one of the wealthiest landowners in Europe.

At twenty, with his mother's blessing and a strong force, the Prince made yet another assault on England and this time he was successful. Stephen was still a fighter but he was growing old and when his own son died, he was ready to come to terms. It was agreed that after Stephen's death, Henry should inherit the kingdom.

A year later, in 1154, Matilda's son was crowned, but the Empress was not present in the Abbey. She refused to return to the land where she had met so many disasters. Instead, she lived to a pious old age at Rouen, although she did not fail to keep an eye on her son's possessions in France nor to send him advice on how to rule the stiff-necked people of England.

HENRY II, THE LAW-GIVER

HENRY inherited his mother's energy but not her arrogance, for he was marvellously humble for so great a monarch. In him there was none of the cruelty of the Norman kings, but at times he showed the almost insane temper of his family.

By a series of fortunate accidents, he was now the most powerful man in Europe for, with Aquitaine from his wife, Normandy and Anjou from his father, and now England, his realms stretched from the borders of Spain to Scotland.

The ruler of these vast possessions was built for the task. His stocky frame, bullet head and open, freckled face revealed the strength and eagerness of a young man bursting with vigour. The terrifying energy that exhausted his courtiers and servants shone from his grey eyes with such brilliance that men came to gaze on him as if, apart from kingship, he was a man above all other humans.

But Henry's gifts were more than those of an athlete and a warrior. He spoke several languages, never forgot a fact or a face, and his knowledge of law was so deep that he was sometimes called upon to settle disputes between foreign princes and cases too difficult for his own judges. He was generous, too, on a kingly scale but, for himself, he cared nothing for clothes or rich living. He would ride for days in the same old tunic and cloak and eat his meals standing up while he read documents or dealt with state business.

Once, the monks of St Swithin at Winchester tearfully complained that their bishop had forbidden three of their dishes at dinner. Henry asked how many dishes they had left and when they answered, 'Only ten,' he replied, 'In my court, I am satisfied with three. I must see that your bishop cuts your dishes to the same.'

Another instance of his rough humour occurred when he was riding with his friend, the great Becket, and they saw a shivering beggar. Turning to his companion, the King asked:

'Would it not be an act of goodness to give that poor man a cloak?'

Becket agreed and Henry cried out, 'Yours be the goodness then!' and flung Becket's fur-lined cloak to the beggar.

But Henry could take a joke against himself. After excommunicating a royal forester, Hugh, Bishop of Lincoln, was summoned to Woodstock Castle, and on arrival he found the King resting from the hunt in a forest glade, surrounded by his courtiers. To show his displeasure, Henry refused to look up or to greet the Bishop,

whereupon Hugh, the bravest of men, shoved a nobleman aside and sat down next to the King. The silence
was unbroken until Henry, who hated to be idle, called
for needle and thread and began to repair a bandage on
his finger. The sewing proceeded in silence. Then Hugh,
leaning sideways, murmured:

'You know, Sire, you remind me of your great-grand-
mother of Falaise.'

Henry's ancestress had been a glove-maker, daughter
of a tanner, and the King, not in the least ashamed of
this fact, burst out laughing:

'Do you not hear what this impudent Bishop said?' he
cried to the courtiers. 'The rogue knows that my great-
grandmother was a woman of the people and he has the
sauce to say that my sewing reminds him of her needle-
craft!'

As soon as he came to the throne, Henry made the

barons pull down their illegal castles and send away the
foreign mercenaries. For the task of restoring law and
order, he chose honest and capable officials, among them
a London merchant's son named Thomas Becket. This
brilliant young man who had been trained for the
Church, rose to become Lord Chancellor and, much to
the disgust of the nobles, the most powerful subject in
the kingdom.

The King and Becket became boon-companions. Both
were tremendous workers; both were masterful charac-
ters; both possessed a deep sense of duty and a love of
justice. The only difference between them was that
whereas Henry cared nothing for his appearance,
Becket, newly arrived at the pinnacle of wealth, loved to
parade his riches and to live in a style far more
magnificent than his royal master.

For several years, the King and his Chancellor
worked together in perfect friendship and when Theo-
bald, the old Archbishop of Canterbury, died in 1161,
it seemed a clever move for Henry to ask the monks to
elect Becket in his place. The highest positions in the
realm – the chancellorship and the head of the Church –
would be in the hands of his most trusted servant.

But Henry had made a mistake. Declaring that he
could not serve two masters, Becket resigned the post of
Chancellor, gave up his magnificent way of life and devoted himself to the service of God and the Church. To
Henry's disgust, he found that he was opposed at every
turn by an Archbishop more rigorous and determined
than any since Anselm.

The fatal clash came over the question of Church
courts. Since William the Conqueror's time, the Church
had possessed the right to try its own wrongdoers in
special Church courts where punishment was much
lighter than in the ordinary courts. Besides priests and

deacons, a huge class of persons could claim to belong to the clergy and the King's judges knew that murderers and thieves were escaping punishment because they lived on Church property or were able to mumble a few words of Latin.

To put an end to this scandal, Henry proposed that after a 'clerk' had been found guilty in a Church court, he should be handed over to a lay court for punishment. In this and in various other matters, Becket refused to budge an inch until the quarrel grew so bitter that he felt obliged to flee abroad.

BECKET AND THE KING

Six years passed until Henry, feeling uneasy at the Pope's displeasure, made peace and Becket returned to Canterbury.

The Archbishop was as obstinate as ever. From his pulpit in the cathedral, he denounced those who had obeyed the King during his absence and he excommunicated several bishops.

The news of this defiance was carried to King Henry in Normandy. Storming up and down in a towering passion, he raged at Becket's treachery and upbraided the cowering nobles:

'What fools and cowards have I nourished in my house that not one will avenge me on this upstart clerk?'

Stung by this taunt, four knights left the hall and took ship to England. At Canterbury, they ordered the Archbishop to keep his word to the King. Becket icily refused and went into the cathedral where the monks were singing vespers. Timidly, they tried to bolt the doors.

'No,' said Becket. 'I will not have God's house turned into a fortress.'

He was moving towards the choir steps when the now armoured knights clattered into the dark cathedral, crying:

'Where is the traitor?'

A clear voice answered them.

'Lo! I am here, no traitor but a priest of God.'

The assassins rushed forwards and thrusting the Archbishop's cross-bearer aside, tried to drag him outside. When he resisted, they lost patience and killed him where he stood on the stone floor of the most holy church in England.

Rightly or wrongly, the blame for the murder was laid on Henry. He walked in penance through the streets and allowed the monks to scourge him at the martyr's tomb; he made gifts and endowed religious houses and he had to give up his plan to reduce the power of the Church.

But if he was defeated here, Henry's desire for justice was unabated and he travelled ceaselessly in order to bring firm government to his vast dominions. In the north, the Scots were cleared from the counties they had taken in Stephen's reign.

In Ireland, once the most godly country in western Europe, there was perpetual warfare between the chieftains. One of these, Dermot of Leinster, rashly invited some of the Norman knights of South Wales to come to help him. Richard of Clare, called Strongbow, restored Dermot to his throne but when he died, Strongbow seized the kingdom. A number of other Norman knights followed suit and set themselves up as rulers in districts that they conquered with their swords.

In 1171 Henry II crossed to Ireland to assert his authority over the knights and their Irish subjects. All accepted him as their lord, but although he set up a government in Dublin, he did not stay long enough to make sure that the nobles ruled the Irish justly.

But Britain was only a part of Henry's domains. To keep any kind of control over the violent nobles of Normandy, Maine, Anjou, Brittany and Aquitaine, he had to travel up and down his territories, dealing out justice and fending off his enemies. The chief of these was the King of France who, at this time, ruled no more than a small area round Paris and looked with envy upon the vast Angevin possessions.

In his almost superhuman task, Henry received little support from his family. Queen Eleanor, a beautiful, tempestuous woman, took herself back to the sunny land of Aquitaine where her court was renowned for the gallantry of its knights and troubadours. Here, she sided with her sons as they grew rebellious against a father who gave them titles but no real power.

In 1178 there was a great rebellion when the eldest son, known as 'the young King Henry' because he had already been crowned, Richard, the second son, and Geoffrey of Brittany, the third, formed an alliance with King Louis VII of France. The Scots and some of the English barons joined the rebels but Henry II was victorious everywhere.

For a few more years he ruled in peace, but although he pardoned his sons, they were soon plotting against him and quarrelling among themselves. 'The young King Henry' died and so did Geoffrey, but Richard, now Duke of Aquitaine, refused to share any of his promised possessions with John, the youngest brother and his father's favourite.

In 1189 Richard again joined forces with King Louis' clever successor, Philip Augustus. Making a sudden attack, they caught Henry unawares and without an army. So many of his castles in Anjou and Touraine were taken that Henry, ill and low-spirited, agreed to accept a humiliating peace. Lying on his bed in his castle at Chinon, he was told that his favourite son John had joined the rebels:

'Is it true that John, my very heart, whom I have loved before all my sons and for whom I have suffered all my ills has deserted me?' he cried in anguish.

When he discovered that John had indeed played him false, he sank back and turned to the wall, crying:

'Now, let all things go, for I care no longer for myself or anything else in the world. Shame, shame upon a conquered king.'

Thus, in bitter despair, the great King died and his son became Richard I of England.

COEUR DE LION

TWO years before Henry's death, the whole of Christendom had been shocked by the news that Saladin, the Muslim leader, had captured Jerusalem. All that remained of the Crusader kingdoms, won by the sword in 1099, was a strip of coast and a few seaports.

The Pope called for a great crusade and the leading monarchs of Europe, the Emperor Frederick Barbarossa, Philip Augustus of France and Henry II, took vows to put aside their rivalries in order to regain the Holy City. But Henry was growing old and his hands were full, so the role of Crusader King fell to his son Richard who was to win the title of *Coeur de Lion* – the Lion Heart.

Richard was now thirty-three, a blond giant who was already renowned as the most chivalrous and skilful

knight in Europe. He had inherited some of his mother's
love of poetry and music but he loved fighting above all
else. Like a gifted sportsman, he was often gallant and
generous to his opponents, but, in other respects, he was
as cruel and greedy as his brothers.

The four months that Richard I lived in England
after his coronation were spent in a frantic endeavour to
raise money for the Crusade. He said that he would sell
the kingdom itself if he could find a buyer but, failing to
do so, he raised large sums by selling offices of state and
granting charters to towns. For 10,000 marks, he released William the Lion from the duty of paying
homage. Then, leaving England in the care of his
mother Eleanor and the Chancellor William Long-
champ, Richard departed for the Holy Land with a
well-equipped army. Unfortunately, he did not take his
brother John with him.

In the company of Philip Augustus, the English King
made a leisurely journey through France and took ship
to the East, pausing on the way to conquer Cyprus, and
to marry Princess Berengaria of Navarre. Meanwhile
Philip Augustus had reached Palestine where a huge
army of Crusaders was besieging the seaport of Acre
with little prospect of success.

Richard's arrival brought zest and an expert knowledge of siege-craft to the scene, and although he fell ill,
he directed operations so forcefully that the town was
captured. The triumph was marred by the massacre of
Saracen prisoners, in revenge, it was said, for a similar
deed by Saladin.

The Crusaders were already at loggerheads. Disease
had killed thousands of the troops; the French and English knights were constantly bickering and Philip
Augustus, irritated by Richard's fame as a soldier, took
himself back to France, promising not to interfere with a

fellow-Crusader's territories. Another enemy was made
when some of Richard's soldiers tore down the flag of
Austria from the walls of Acre and trampled it under-
foot. Vowing to have his revenge one day, Leopold of
Austria also quitted the Crusade.

Richard stayed on. He routed Saladin's army at
Arsouf, captured Jaffa and pressed on towards Jerusalem. But a European army was ill-equipped to
march, let alone to fight, in a land where the heat and
lack of water were tortures to men in armour. Each night
the Crusaders knelt and stretched out their arms towards
Jerusalem, crying:

'Help us! Holy Sepulchre, help us!'

But they never reached the Holy City, for Richard
was forced to order his dwindling army to retreat. He
made a treaty with Saladin that saved the pilgrim's
route and the remnant of the Crusader kingdoms for
another fifty years. Then, in 1192, having heard alarm-
ing news about the league between his brother John and
Philip Augustus, he set out for home.

Since it would be dangerous to go through France,
Richard decided to sail up the Adriatic to Venice. His
ship was wrecked and he was making his way overland,
disguised as a merchant, when he was recognized near
Vienna. He was arrested and taken before his old enemy,
Duke Leopold of Austria, who gleefully handed him
over to the Emperor.

During his captivity in Germany, Richard wrote
songs and set them to music. For a time, no one knew
where he was imprisoned and there may well be truth in
the romantic story of Blondel the minstrel, trudging
from castle to castle, seeking his master by singing Aquitaine songs until an answering voice from a barred
window told him where the royal prisoner lay.

After hard bargaining, during which John and Philip

Augustus did their best to prevent Richard's release, the English people raised an enormous ransom for the hero-King whom they had hardly set eyes on. In March 1194, Richard was free and on his way to London when Philip sent an urgent message to John:

'Look to yourself for the Great Devil himself is unchained!'

John fled but soon afterwards Richard pardoned his brother, saying contemptuously, 'You are but a child.' But he had no mind to forgive Philip Augustus. Within a few months, he had raised an army and had crossed the Channel to try to recover his lost possessions. He never returned.

Great soldier as he was, Richard found it difficult to pin down a wily enemy. He won victories and built his famous fortress, Saucy Castle, to guard the border of Normandy, but the cost of the Crusade and the ransom had exhausted England, so that he was constantly short of the men and supplies which he needed for final success.

In 1199 Richard was at Chalus, besieging a vassal

who refused to hand over some treasure found on his land. The castle was weakly held and Richard, unarmoured, was watching his men make short work of its defences when a crossbowman on the wall took careful aim and fired a bolt that struck him in the chest. The castle was stormed and the soldier who had shot him was taken before the dying King:

'What have I done to thee that thou shouldst slay me?' asked Richard.

'Thou hast killed my father and two of my brothers,' replied the bowman. 'I shall die gladly knowing that I have slain thee.'

The King ordered the man to be set free and shortly afterwards, urging his barons to accept John as his successor, he died. To their shame, his soldiers seized the crossbowman and, ignoring Richard's last order, put him to a horrible death.

KING JOHN

JOHN was not the nearest to the throne by birth, for his elder brother, Geoffrey, had left a son named Prince Arthur of Brittany. However, Arthur was only a boy and old Queen Eleanor and the barons gave their support to John.

The new King had always been the problem-child of his family. At his birth, his father called him John Lackland because the royal possessions had already been promised to the three older sons and it was Henry II's efforts to provide a share for 'Lackland' that had led to the family quarrels.

Cherished by a doting father and despised by his brothers, John grew into a talented youth whose good looks were spoiled by an expression of wolfish cunning. He made a fool of himself when he was sent to Ireland to complete its conquest, and later he broke his father's heart and betrayed his brother. Yet there were times when he could show the volcanic energy and warlike skill of Richard, and he had far more understanding of the way to rule a kingdom than his famous brother. He was a failure because no one could love him. He was utterly faithless and earned the hatred of everyone except his foreign mercenaries.

At first John did well. He visited his dominions in France and overawed the barons who had been prepared to support Prince Arthur and laid siege to Queen Eleanor in one of her castles, John raced to his mother's rescue with such astounding speed that he took the beseigers by surprise, routed them and captured Arthur himself.

No one knew exactly what happened to the young Prince. Some said that he was blinded and hidden away but it seems more likely that he was murdered at Rouen, probably by John himself in a fit of drunken rage.

The crime did great harm to John. As the French mounted fresh attacks on Normandy, his allies and the Norman barons deserted him. Paralysed, it seemed, by a strange idleness, he did little to save the Duchy, only muttering as news came in that yet another castle had fallen:

'Let be, let be. One day I shall win it all again.'

The truth was that his forces were so honeycombed with treachery that he could trust no one. Normandy was lost and John went back to England where his energy returned like a flood. He toured the country ceaselessly, seldom staying more than a day in one place, but wherever he went he sat in the law-courts, forced his officials to work as never before, ordered good coins to be minted, granted charters to growing towns, built a navy and, sometimes, was generous to the poor.

Although his chief aim was to enrich himself, John provided firm government until his disastrous quarrel with the Church. He ordered the Canterbury monks to choose one of his friends as their Archbishop but, on the Pope's advice, they elected Stephen Langton, an English cardinal living abroad. John angrily drove out the monks and seized their property:

'As for Langton,' he cried, 'I will hang him by the neck if he so much as sets foot in my kingdom!'

The Pope's answer was to punish the people of England. The churches were closed, and presently John himself was excommunicated; but, to the horror of most

men, he gleefully rifled the Church treasures, and with the proceeds hired an army to attack William the Lion of Scotland.

He defeated the Scots, the Welsh and the Irish chieftains, and appeared to be triumphant everywhere. Then the Pope directed that this godless King must be removed from his throne by the Church's champion, Philip Augustus.

The French King was collecting an invasion force when John turned the tables on his enemy. Inviting Stephen Langton to England, he made his peace with the Church by kneeling humbly before the Archbishop and by actually surrendering England to the Pope.

Exulting at his own cleverness, John now ordered his barons to join him in a great attack on France. When they refused, he sailed with a hired army but, on the continent, his allies collapsed and he came home to face a rebellion.

The King's greed and cruelty, his mocking insults and his habit of giving the chief posts of honour to foreign

ruffians had destroyed the barons' loyalty. In 1215 they
rode to London and drew up a charter of their rights
which, they insisted, the King must accept.

John, having paid off his mercenaries, was at Windsor
with only a small bodyguard. When he heard of the
barons' demands, he burst out:

'They might as well ask for my crown!'

On 15th June he was forced to meet his opponents in a
field called Runnymeade where, under a silk awning, he
sullenly put his seal to the Great Charter, promising to
rule according to the laws and customs of the realm.

John had no intention of keeping his word and when
he had obtained a letter from the Pope freeing him from
the Charter, he hired an army and cried balefully:

'Now, by God's teeth, I will make my barons howl for
mercy. Before this year is out, there will be so little left in
the land that men will pay a shilling for a halfpenny
loaf!'

He struck like a hurricane, sweeping across the
country to capture his enemies' castles and to ravage
their estates. In the wake of his army trundled a line of
wagons creaking with the weight of the barons' treasures. In despair, the barons invited Louis of France,
Philip's son, to come with arms to be their king. In 1216
a French army landed and all that summer there was
civil war in England.

In October, after a series of masterly manoeuvres,
John was in Lincolnshire, harrying the land where the
corn was still uncut. He doubled back to Lynn, near the
Wash and then, although unwell, he set out for the north
again, ordering his baggage train to take a short cut
across the river-estuary at low tide. This was a well-
known route but one of the leading wagons stuck and the
others, halted, became bogged down. The sea came
racing in before they could be freed and John, watching

in agony from the Lincolnshire side, saw his entire baggage train swept away.

To a man who loved jewels and gold as much as John,
this was a terrible blow but to a king waging war with
hired foreigners, it was disaster. Numb with despair, he
rode to Sleaford where, said the monks afterwards, he
made himself ill by overeating; but he was already sick
and broken in spirit. Carried by litter to Newark Castle,
John died there on 19th October, 1216, and a few days
later at Gloucester his nine-year-old son was proclaimed
Henry III. As the royal regalia had been lost, the boy
was crowned with a plain gold circlet provided by his
mother.

HENRY III AND THE BARONS

THE crowning of young Henry did not bring peace immediately. Louis and his supporters were supreme in the south, except at Dover where Hubert de Burgh was heroically holding out in the castle; but those who had hated John had no quarrel with his little son and many began to change sides.

When William Marshall, an aged baron and the most honourable man in England, routed Louis' troops at Lincoln, and the dauntless Hubert de Burgh took to the sea to defeat a French fleet off Sonwith, Louis gave up the struggle and retired to his own country.

For the next two years, the country was ruled by William Marshall, and after his death by Hubert de Burgh, the justiciar or chief minister. Hubert took on the task of destroying or taking for the King the numerous castles that had been built during the civil war. More troublesome were John's foreign friends such as Peter des Roches and Falkes de Bréauté, an engaging rascal who had amassed a fortune. In 1224 Hubert captured Bedford Castle, Falkes' chief stronghold, and put an end, for the time being, to the power of the foreign adventurers.

Meanwhile Henry III was growing up and, when at the age of twenty this learned youth became King, it was evident that he had inherited none of his father's wickedness – nor any of his ability to rule.

Henry III's reign was a glorious period for religion and the arts. Beautiful churches and cathedrals were built, colleges were founded and the poor friars arrived in England to win widespread love and support; but the pious, generous King was also an extravagant weakling who ruled badly.

Hubert de Burgh was dismissed and treated like a criminal in return for his great services, while Peter des Roches came back from exile to win such influence over the King that he and his friends obtained most of the chief positions in the realm.

The barons, who now regarded themselves as Englishmen, protested so hotly against these foreigners that Henry agreed to dismiss des Roches and his hangers-on. Unfortunately, the King did not learn his lesson. After his marriage to Eleanor of Provence, he rewarded droves of her needy relations.

In addition, he annoyed his own people by allowing the Pope to impose heavy taxes and to fill many places in the English Church with French and Italian priests.

Henry, who acted as his own chancellor and treasurer, decided to invade France to recover his father's lost possessions, but the attempt was a failure. Just as expensive was his foolish plan to have his second son made King of Sicily. By this time, the King was bankrupt and his nobles were ready to revolt.

The barons found a leader in Simon de Montfort, Earl of Leicester who, oddly enough, was himself a foreigner, married to the King's sister. However, Simon's good qualities had won wide respect and he was one of the members of the council, or parliament that met at Oxford to discuss the King's mismanagement. Henry reluctantly agreed to mend his ways, but hating the idea of taking orders from a council, he soon obtained the Pope's permission to break his word.

At this, the barons took up arms and in the Barons' War that followed, Simon de Montfort became their acknowledged leader, while the King's eldest son, 'the Lord Edward', commanded his father's forces.

After some royalist successes, the two sides met in strength at Lewes where Prince Edward dashed so vigorously at the Londoners that he drove them headlong from the field. In his absence, de Montfort won the battle and captured King Henry so that when Edward returned, he could do no more than give himself up as a hostage.

De Montfort's victory prompted him to summon the Parliament of 1265. This was no more than a gathering of his own supporters. Few of the nobles attended, but besides the clergy and the two knights from each shire, there were representatives from various towns and cities. Thus, because he called on ordinary citizens – the commons – to take a share in governing the country, Simon de Montfort is often looked upon as the founder of the House of Commons.

Yet the Earl's power slipped away as soon as he grasped it. He held the affection of the Londoners and the common people, but the nobles came to hate him as an arrogant upstart. Thus, when Prince Edward escaped from captivity, he was able to raise a large army and to overwhelm de Montfort at Evesham, where 'the good Earl', as the people called him, was killed.

With the opposition beaten and his capable son in charge of the kingdom, Henry III lived out the last seven years of his reign in peace. Indeed, Prince Edward restored order so well that he felt able to take the Cross and to sail to the east on a Crusade. By now the days of the great Crusades were over and the Prince found little chance to win renown apart from a dramatic escape from death. An assassin stabbed him with a poisoned dagger, and it is said that his devoted young wife, Princess Eleanor, saved him by sucking the poison from the wound.

The Prince had reached Sicily on his way home when he learned that his father had died and that he was Edward I of England.

ROGER BACON, THE LEARNED FRIAR

DURING Henry III's reign, a clever youngster came up from Somerset to the university at Oxford. He was Roger Bacon, son of a well-to-do landowner, and he sat at the feet of Robert Grosseteste, a man of the most delightful character, who had risen from a peasant's upbringing to become one of the greatest scholars of the age.

After Grosseteste had left Oxford to become Bishop of Lincoln, Bacon continued his studies in Paris where he was able to make experiments and to talk with scholars from many countries – Arab mathematicians, Jewish physicians, Italian astronomers and doctors.

But although Bacon had a brilliant mind, his sharp tongue and his interest in strange forms of learning brought him into trouble. He believed that in the search for knowledge he need not follow the well-worn paths of logic and scripture but that he should study the marvels of the world about him – sunlight, stars, rainbows, plants, chemicals and gases.

When his outspoken opinions made him unpopular in Paris, Bacon returned to Oxford where he joined the

Order of St. Francis. The Franciscans were well known for their interest in learning and Bacon may have entered the Order partly as a protection against his enemies. At all events, students crowded to listen to the brilliant friar who had so many novel ideas that they called him 'the Marvellous Doctor'. He despised the way in which most scholars decided all kinds of difficult problems by merely talking about them, for he preferred to discover facts by observation and experiment:

'There are two ways of gaining knowledge,' he said. 'Argument and experience. Argument gives no proof nor does it remove doubt, unless the truth is discovered by way of experience.'

So he made calculations, heated substances and weighed them; he invented a magnifying-glass, a telescope to study the stars, and, it was rumoured, gunpowder. Strange bubblings and explosions were heard at night from 'Friar Bacon's Tower' where he lived, and people began to wonder if he was dabbling in the black arts. Was he perhaps the servant of the Devil?

When Bacon refused to give up these experiments, he was exiled to Paris and deprived of all his books and instruments. Luckily a Franciscan, who had formerly listened to his lectures with admiration, became Pope Clement IV and sent a message to the unhappy scholar asking him to write a book about his opinions. Bacon was overjoyed and immediately began to set down his beliefs and discoveries in science, anatomy, medicine and music. It was an immense task but at last the book was finished.

'It is done,' he wrote to the Pope. 'I have written what I believe to be the truth and I have called it my Great Work.'

Unfortunately, the Pope died before he could study the masterpiece and it was not long before Bacon was again accused of practising witchcraft. In 1277 he was arrested and thrown into prison.

Fourteen years passed and it was not until he was almost eighty that the broken old man was allowed to return to Oxford to die.

'They have treated me like a criminal,' he said, 'but all my life I have only been a seeker after knowledge while they stood in the way of the light.'

EDWARD I, 'THE HAMMER OF THE SCOTS'

THE son of Henry III was as upright and unbending as a lance. At thirty-three, when he became King, Edward was one of the tallest and most handsome men in the land and his talents matched his splendid appearance. Moreover, he had seen his father's faults and he had learned what a King must do to hold his power and to keep the respect of his people.

His first task was to subdue the Welsh. During the Barons' Wars Llewelyn ap Griffith, a supporter of de Montfort, had made himself so powerful that he was recognized as Prince of Wales and overlord of all the lesser chieftains. However, Llewelyn's own feudal lord was the King of England and, in accordance with custom, he was summoned to Westminster to take the oath of loyalty to the new King.

Llewelyn refused to go, making excuses that did not hide his intention to set himself up as an independent ruler. Edward was patient but, at last, feeling that one disobedient vassal would encourage others, he invaded Wales in 1277, striking with three armies at the south, the centre and the north. Llewelyn, a brave and resourceful leader, was blockaded in the rocky wastes of Snowdon until hunger and cold forced him to surrender.

Edward treated the Welsh prince mildly. He made him do homage in London so that all men should know that he had acknowledged his overlord. Llewelyn had to give back the territories gained during Henry III's reign, but he was allowed to keep his title of Prince and to return to North Wales.

It was not long before the harsh behaviour of Edward's officials caused the Welsh to take up arms. Llewelyn and his brother David were the natural leaders of the revolt in the north and they were supported by risings throughout the whole of Wales.

When Edward again led his army towards Snowdon, Llewelyn had no intention of being trapped a second time. He broke through the English lines and was on his way to join the rebels in the south when he was slain in a chance encounter with some enemy troops.

David held out in the mountains for another year, but after he was captured and executed at Shrewsbury,

Edward decided to put an end to the troubles with the Welsh. Dividing the principality into five shires, he set up English government and laws and surrounded Snowdon, the refuge of the rebels, with a ring of massive fortresses. In one of these, Caernarvon Castle, his son Edward was born and presented, it is said, to the Welsh chieftains as 'a prince born in Wales, unable to speak a word of English'.

Later, when the boy was seventeen, the King conferred on him the title of Prince of Wales and whether or not this gesture pleased the Welsh, they remained quiet for another century.

Edward I was a masterly soldier but his true greatness was as a ruler. He gave his people a series of laws that

improved justice by abolishing many of the barons' private courts, and by rooting out dishonest sheriffs and judges. He encouraged the wool trade with Flanders and kept the barons in a state, not of fear, but of respect and obedience.

It is curious that Edward was honoured for an act that nowadays would be regarded as inhumanly cruel. The Jews, ill-treated and despised for centuries, were able to exist only by lending money, an occupation forbidden to Christians. Most kings, being perpetually short of money, protected the Jews when it suited them to do so and afterwards taxed them cruelly and confiscated their wealth. Edward, feeling that it would be sinful to borrow money from the Jews, expelled all of them from the country in 1290.

Had Edward's reign ended in 1295, the year of the Model Parliament, it would have been a period of unbroken success, but the last twelve years of his life were spent in a costly struggle with the Scots that led to centuries of bitterness between the two peoples.

In 1286, when Alexander III was killed and his granddaughter, the Maid of Norway, died on the voyage to her kingdom, the royal line of Scotland came to an end and no fewer than thirteen nobles put in claims to the throne. The most notable were John Balliol and Robert Bruce, both descended from William the Lion's brother and both having estates in England for which they paid homage to Edward I.

The English King was invited to judge the various claims to the throne, and although this seemed to be a sensible way of avoiding civil war, the Scots were startled when he insisted that they should first do homage to him. However, they consented, and after a careful hearing Edward awarded the throne to John Balliol.

From the beginning, Balliol appeared to be no more

than a puppet and the Scottish nobles felt that they had
been tricked over the act of homage. Thus, when
Edward summoned them to serve him in a quarrel with
France, they not only refused but made an alliance with
the French.

At this, Edward led an army into Scotland, defeated
the Scots at Dunbar, removed Balliol from the throne
and carried the coronation stone from Scone to Westminster to show that he intended to rule the country
himself. Having, as he thought, settled the matter, he
gave his attention to affairs in France and to a squabble
with some of the English nobles who did not want to
fight for him on the Continent.

Meanwhile, although most of the Scottish nobles had
made their peace with Edward, the Lowlanders were
becoming fiercely indignant at the arrogance of the
English garrison troops. One day a Scottish gentleman
named William Wallace was roughly handled by a
company of English soldiers. He defended himself and,
in the scuffle, killed one of the attackers. Wallace went
into hiding but, learning that his home had been sacked
and his young wife murdered, he swore never to sheath
his sword until he had taken vengeance on his country's
oppressors.

Joined by a few fellow-outlaws and then by increasing
numbers of small landowners and peasants, Wallace
built up a force that became strong enough to harry the
English troops, to capture several castles and to win a
major victory at Stirling Bridge.

Edward I, who had been fighting in Flanders, hurried
home and routed the Scots at Falkirk. Wallace escaped
from the field, but some time afterwards he was betrayed by the sheriff of Dumbarton and carried to
London to be executed. The four quarters of his brave
body were sent to Scotland to be shown in the chief

towns as a warning, but instead, they kindled a passionate spirit for independence.

During these stirring events, Robert Bruce, the twenty-five-year-old grandson of the claimant, had been living at the English court where he had served Edward I and had fought in his army. Roused perhaps by Wallace's example, he made his way to Scotland where he met Red Comyn, one of the Scottish leaders, in a church at Dumfries. Suspecting that Comyn was playing a double game, Bruce angrily upbraided him and, in the quarrel drew a dagger and killed him.

Aghast at his crime, Bruce fled to the hills but presently, setting himself up as a new champion, he revived his family claim to the throne and had himself crowned at Scone.

With few supporters and no money or influence, Bruce seemed to be courting disaster. His wife and his daughter were arrested, his friends were executed and an English army scattered his meagre force so that he became a fugitive living perilously in the mountains with a handful of followers.

For a time Bruce seemed to be no more than a nuisance to the occupying forces, but as his following grew, he was able to make serious raids on the enemy and he had the advantage of being always able to retreat into the inaccessible moors and forests of the Highlands. As one success followed another, his force grew into a sizeable army and Edward I felt that it was time that he himself dealt with this rebel leader.

The King was now almost seventy and his huge frame was worn out after a lifetime of ceaseless activity, but, determined as ever, he set out to conquer Scotland for the third time. In 1307, too weak to ride but carried in a litter at the head of his army, the old warrior was nearing the Border when he died.

EDWARD II

CONFIDENT that he understood his son's character, the dying King made Prince Edward swear to continue the war until Robert Bruce was defeated, but the handsome, feckless Prince was already tired of army life. He scurried back to London where he dismissed his father's most trusted ministers and recalled from exile his former playfellow, a conceited young Gascon named Piers Gaveston.

Edward II speedily aroused the barons' dislike by pouring gifts and honours into the hands of Gaveston. Moreover, he and his favourite took a delight in mocking the nobles as 'the Hog', 'the Black Dog of Arden' and 'the Cuckoo'.

At length, the enraged nobles formed a committee

called the Lords Ordainers who took over the government and banished Gaveston from the realm. When
Edward recalled his crony and sent him for safety to
Scarborough Castle, the Earl of Warwick, 'the Black
Dog', brought up an army and forced Gaveston to surrender. Having captured the detested Gascon, the nobles
were in no mind to let him escape – 'If you let the fox go,
you have to hunt him again,' so Gaveston's head was
struck off.

For the moment, Edward was powerless to revenge his
friend's murder, especially as affairs in Scotland were
now in a critical state.

Robert Bruce had taken full advantage of the quarrels
between King and barons in England. He united his
countrymen and raised an army to ravage the English
counties of the north. Then he began a systematic attack
on Edward I's castles in the Lowlands. Perth, Roxburgh,
Edinburgh and Linlithgow were captured, and by 1314
only Stirling was holding out. Its governor was so hard
pressed that he agreed to surrender if help had not
arrived by 24th June.

If Stirling fell, English rule in Scotland would be
ended and even Edward II felt that he must bestir himself. A great army was hurriedly raised and it arrived
within sight of Stirling only one day before the promised
date of surrender.

At Bannockburn the English found that Bruce was
waiting to fight in a place of his own choosing. The
position was fearsomely strong, but there was no time for
the English to manoeuvre and, in any case, their army
seemed to be overwhelmingly powerful.

But Edward II's presence meant that there was no real
general in command and his discontented nobles seemed
to have forgotten any of the lessons in warfare that they
should have learned under the old King.

On the evening before the battle there was a dramatic incident when Sir Henry Bohun, eager to destroy the Scottish King in single combat, dashed from a company of English horsemen who were examining the Scottish position. Bruce, mounted on a pony, was inspecting his troops when he looked up to see an adversary thundering towards him with levelled lance. At the last instant, Bruce wheeled his pony aside and, rising in his stirrups, crashed his axe down upon the knight's head. The steel helmet split in two and Bohun fell lifeless from the saddle.

'I have broken my good axe,' was all that Bruce said as he returned to his cheering countrymen.

On the morrow, the English archers were sent so far ahead of the cavalry that the Scottish horsemen were able to destroy them from the flank. After this stupid misuse of the archers, Edward's mail-clad knights made a massed charge at the enemy. But the square of Scottish spearmen stood firm, thrusting away at the chargers to bring down horses and riders, so that the English, with little enough room to move in, were hampered by the plunging masses of maddened horses and fallen men. Even so, weight of numbers might have told but for the unexpected arrival of a new army advancing with banners, a little to the rear of the Scottish position. In reality, these were no more than camp-followers who, in their excitement, dashed forward with wild shouts of 'Slay! Slay!'

Panic spread through the English ranks and, as Bruce ordered an advance, they broke in a headlong rout and perished by the thousand as they floundered in the marshy ground and stumbled into the pits that Bruce had dug to protect his flank. Edward II was among the few who fled fast enough to escape from the scene of the greatest English defeat since Hastings.

Stirling Castle surrendered and English rule of Scotland came to an end, leaving Bruce free to govern his own countrymen, and to ravage the north of England year in and year out.

The defeat at Bannockburn had been stained by the King's cowardice and Edward II was now a man despised by all, including his wife Isabella of France, the most beautiful Queen in Europe. He could not defend his people in the north, and two years of famine and disastrous rains caused widespread suffering and discontent. Yet, in their opposition to the King, the Lords Ordainers had no thought for the common people but only of their own advantage.

From this welter of greed and treachery, Edward suddenly struck out with unexpected energy. Aided by his new favourites the Dispensers, father and son, he defeated and executed his chief opponent, Henry of Lancaster, overthrew the Ordainers and took the government into his own hands.

The Dispensers were capable men but their arrogance and greed had already brought hatred upon themselves and their master when a fresh calamity overwhelmed the King.

Queen Isabella and her fourteen-year-old son, Prince Edward, made a visit to Paris where Isabella fell in love with Roger Mortimer, an exiled nobleman who loathed the Dispensers. In 1326 Isabella and Mortimer landed in Suffolk, declaring that they had come to rid the country of the King's unpopular favourites. Edward II, having lost the respect of all classes, found himself deserted. He fled to Wales but was tracked down and captured. Forced to give up his crown to his son, the wretched man was treated with savage contempt and, after being dragged from one prison to another, he was finally murdered by his enemies in Berkeley Castle.

For three years Isabella and Mortimer ruled in the name of young Edward III until, in 1330, when he had almost grown to manhood, Edward's eyes were opened to his mother's disgraceful position and to the greedy insolence of her partner. One night supported by a party of soldiers who entered Nottingham Castle by a secret passage, Edward seized Mortimer and, ignoring the Queen's cry of 'Fair son, have pity on the gentle Mortimer,' sent the favourite to be hanged at Tyburn like a common thief. Then he ordered his mother to a country manor where she was made to spend the rest of her life in retirement.

EDWARD III

EDWARD III appeared to be the perfect monarch.
Tall, vigorous and handsome, he was a born soldier and
a chivalrous knight whose courtesy to the greatest and
humblest of his subjects seemed to spring from a noble
nature set far above the common rank. Yet Edward
cared little for the good of his people. For him they
existed in order to provide him with the money and men
for the dearest object in life, the winning of glory on the
field of battle.

At first Edward tried to recover Scotland, where
Bruce had died, leaving his crown to his small son,
David. The English King succeeded in putting John
Balliol's son on the throne and he defeated the Scots at
Halidon Hill, but although young David had to flee to

France, the Scots refused to be conquered. They managed to hold out until Edward was drawn into a war that seemed to offer far more attractive opportunities for an accomplished knight.

The French had been helping the Scots by attacking Gascony, the English King's possession in south-west France; in retaliation, Edward supported the people of Flanders who were at loggerheads with their overlord, the King of France. Edward also remembered that he could claim the French crown through his mother, Queen Isabella, sister of Charles IV who had recently died.

Taking the title 'King of France', therefore, Edward prepared for war with the enthusiastic support of his people who expected unlimited opportunities for glory, trade and loot.

The war opened in 1340 when, at Sluys off the coast of

Flanders, the English won a notable sea-battle that gave
them command of the Channel for many years. After a
seige or two, with some fighting in Brittany and Gascony
and the usual burning and looting, both sides agreed to a
truce in order to build up fresh reserves of money and
supplies.

In 1346 Edward's commander in Gascony was hard
pressed, so the King invaded Normandy as a diversion.
Accompanied by his sixteen-year-old son, the Prince of
Wales (later called the Black Prince), he captured Caen
and advanced into France. He had sacked several towns
when he became aware that his army was being tracked
by an enormous host of Frenchmen led by Philip VI.

Putting on speed, Edward marched north in the hope
of joining his Flemish allies but, having forced his way
across the Somme, he was brought to bay near the
village of Crecy. There, with his general's eye, he chose a
sloping piece of ground that was ideal for the kind of
battle that he intended to fight.

The English army consisted of men-at-arms who dis-
mounted and sent their horses to the rear, and archers
armed with the longbow. This weapon had been
developed in Wales and used during the Scottish wars
until, in the hands of practised bowmen, it was now the
deadliest weapon in existence.

On 26th August the French attacked. Their Genoese
crossbowmen wilted under a hail of arrows and were
ridden down by the impatient French knights who
charged uphill and perished in thousands through their
own recklessness and the unerring skill of the English
archers.

For a time the Prince of Wales on the right was hard
pressed when the French came to grips with their
enemy. He was knocked over but Sir Richard Fitz-
Simon, covering the boy with a standard, straddled his

body and roared 'Edward! Edward! St. George to Edward!' so valiantly that the mace-swinging Bishop of Durham crashed to the rescue. To the satisfaction of the King, watching coolly from a windmill, the lad regained his foothold and in the end the battle was won.

The destruction of the French army opened the road to Calais where Edward was angered by having to waste a year in starving the seaport into surrender. In the besiegers' town that grew up outside the walls, the King's court was enlivened by the arrival of Queen Philippa and many ladies from England, together with merchants and shopkeepers.

When the port finally surrendered, Edward was in no mood to treat the common townsfolk with the chivalry that he would have shown to noblemen. He had lost hundreds of soldiers from camp-sickness and the siege had cost him time and money. It was enough to spare most of the gaunt survivors and he ordered the leading burghers to be hanged like criminals as a warning to other towns that might refuse to yield.

It was at this point that Queen Philippa won the astonished admiration of Europe by pleading on her knees for the lives of six men whose claim to mercy was not noble birth but courage. To Edward's credit, he sighed, 'Ah lady, for the love I bear you, I cannot refuse. Take them and do with them as you please.'

In the following year a ship docked at Weymouth carrying, in the bodies of the black rats in its hold, a disease known as the Black Death which raged across England for two years. How many people died cannot be calculated. Probably a third of the population perished, not only in the densely packed towns but in the monasteries, hamlets and villages.

The effect of this disaster was worst in the country districts, for although trade and manufactures were in-

creasing, wealth was still chiefly in land and in the food
that it produced. In places there were not enough men
left alive to plough the fields or to gather the harvest;
wages went up steeply despite the efforts of Parliament
to peg them down, and a bitter enmity arose between the
peasants and their lords.

THE BLACK PRINCE

IN 1355 the French war began again when the Black Prince landed an army at Bordeaux, the wine-city of English-held France. Joined by the Gascon knights, he made a three months' tour pillaging and devastating the lovely countryside as far south as the Mediterranean coast.

Next year the Prince ventured into the heart of France with no more than 12,000 men. Expecting that his father and Lancaster would strike from north and west to join him, he harried the land at his leisure and then, receiving no news of his father, turned south again with his plunder-laden wagons. He did not know until it was almost too late that a huge French army was bearing down on his small force.

Near Poitiers the Prince was caught and hemmed in. So hopeless was his position that he offered to hand over all his prisoners and loot and to give a solemn promise not to fight again for seven years.

John, the French King who had succeeded his father
Philip IV, refused to accept these terms, for he and
his nobles welcomed the opportunity to wipe out the
memory of Crecy.

The battle of Poitiers took place on a slope where the
English archers had the cover of a long hedge and
vineyards. Remembering Crecy, the French advanced on
foot, but, by the time they had trudged half a mile uphill
in stifling heat and in heavy armour, much of their
vigour was spent. Yard-long arrows sped pitilessly into
their crowded ranks and, after the Dauphin's division
was beaten and the Duke of Orleans' arms had quitted
the field without striking a blow, the Prince boldly
advanced upon King John's division, while his Gascon
cavalry made a surprise flank attack.

Although King John and his little son Philip fought
with splendid courage, the boy following his father and
crying, 'Guard on the right, father! Guard on the left!',
both were taken prisoner.

Edward III now advanced to Paris across a countryside terribly devastated by war. Both sides were exhausted and, in 1360, they agreed to stop fighting. Edward
gave up his claim to the French throne in return for wide
possessions including Aquitaine, Gascony and Calais.
King John was released but, finding that his vast ransom
could not be raised, he honourably returned to captivity
and died in London in 1364.

Meanwhile, Prince Edward – the Black Prince – and
his wife Joan, the Fair Maid of Kent, had gone to live in
Aquitaine where, at Bordeaux, they set up a most
brilliant court. Bored by this glittering but peaceful
existence, the Prince led an army into Spain to assist
Pedro the Cruel, the King of Castile, who had recently
been driven from his throne.

By a brilliant victory at Najara, Prince Edward put

the tyrant back on his throne, only to find that Pedro
had no intention of paying his ally or giving him any
assistance. Heavily in debt, his army riddled by a disease which he himself caught, Edward returned to Aquitaine where some of his subjects were in a state of
rebellion.

Under its new King, Charles V, France was recovering. Bertrand du Guesclin, a soldier of genius, realized
that the English could be beaten by new tactics. In place
of the vast, unwieldy armies, small forces of professional
soldiers took the field against the English, nibbling away
at their territories and avoiding pitched battles in order
to garrison towns that were ready to throw off the
foreign yoke.

One of these towns was Limoges and, although Prince
Edward was so ill that he could not ride a horse, he
vowed to punish the townsfolk. He captured Limoges
and ordered all the inhabitants to be put to the sword.
The massacre went on until, seeing a small group of
knights defending themselves with the utmost bravery,
Edward relented and ordered the killing to stop.

Soon afterwards, the Prince returned to England in
hope of recovering but, although he lingered sufficiently
long to show that he would have made a far better ruler
than his father, his illness grew worse and he died in
1376 at Berkhampsted Castle. During his absence, all
the English possessions in France were lost, apart from a
few coast towns. By the end of the Black Prince's life,
Crecy and Poitiers had been fully avenged.

At home, as abroad, the early glories of Edward III's
reign had faded. The defeats in France, the King's de-
cline into a feeble old age, the Prince's illness and his
quarrels with his brother, John of Gaunt, made a dismal
contrast to the days of brilliant achievement.

There was nothing to show for all the blood and gold

that had been spent and, as the King lost control of affairs and the nobles jostled each other in a spiteful struggle for power, the common people looked on the government and the Church with glowering discontent.

The poet Chaucer had criticized the clergy who were lazy and dishonest, but in a poem of the time called *Piers Plowman*, William Langland expressed a savage contempt for churchmen who ignored the suffering of the poor. In this bitter atmosphere John Wycliffe and his wandering preachers, the Lollards, found eager listeners when they attacked the wickedness of the clergy and the nobles.

RICHARD II AND THE PEASANTS

IN 1377, when Edward III died, the Black Prince's son, Richard II, was only eleven years old, and a council of nobles was appointed to rule the country until he came of age. Early in the reign, in order to pay for the French War, the government levied a poll-tax, i.e. a tax on every poll or head in the realm; this tax fell heaviest upon the poor, who were already in a dangerous mood.

Despite Parliament's order, wages had gone up, and in many ways the peasants were better off than before the Black Death, but they were not entirely free. Some of them still had to pay fines when a parent died or a daughter married; some were still forced to grind their corn in the lord's mill and to bake their bread in the lord's oven and to pay for the privilege. All of them hated the name of 'serf' and the threat of bondage.

On the village greens, they listened to Lollards preaching about the sinfulness of great riches, and in the taverns they chuckled over the popular rhymes that mocked the nobles. They passed on secret messages from their brothers in distant counties and they muttered the famous rhyme of John Ball 'the mad priest of Kent':

'When Adam delved and Eve span
Who was then the gentleman?'

The spark that set light to this smouldering discontent was the murder of a tax-collector in Kent by Wat Tyler, a brawny ex-soldier, who quickly found himself at the head of an army of angry Kentishmen.

Having freed John Ball from jail, the peasants

marched on London to lay their troubles before the young King and to rid him of the evil counsellors who, they declared, were the cause of the country's misfortunes. All along the route, villagers and townsfolk left their work to join the ranks, often pausing to take a quick revenge on a harsh steward or a luckless lawyer. Messengers sped ahead to carry the tidings of revolt to the men of Essex, Hertfordshire, Surrey and Norfolk.

The peasants were 'seekers of truth and justice, not thieves or robbers', cried Wat Tyler but, once inside the gates of London, he was unable to control the riff-raff that tagged alongside his followers. Savoy Palace, the princely home of John of Gaunt, went up in flames; merchants' houses were broken into, swords were drawn and a lawless mob began to loot and kill with frantic greed. While the nobles were paralysed with fear, a party of bold peasants forced a way into the Tower and murdered the Archbishop of Canterbury and the Lord Treasurer.

Meanwhile, the young King, showing more courage than his ministers, faced the rebels and promised to grant them their freedom if they would go quietly home. Thirty clerks sat up all night writing out pardons, and many of the peasants were already trudging back to their villages when Wat Tyler and his army met the King at Smithfield, outside the city walls.

During the parley some of the King's party shouted abuse at Tyler who leaned forward to speak to Richard; whereupon William Walworth, the Lord Mayor, either from anger or from fear for the young King's safety, drew his dagger and stabbed Tyler.

'They have slain our captain!' roared the peasants, but the nerve of the boy King prevented a massacre. Riding forward, he cried:

'I am your captain and your King! Follow me!'

At this, the peasants lowered their weapons and presently made off home, cheerfully trusting in the renewed promises of pardon and freedom.

But once the danger was over, the nobles took a swift revenge for the fright they had suffered. With their soldiers, they hunted down the ringleaders and hanged them in market squares and at abbey gates, while the four quarters of John Ball's body were carted from town to town. As their leaders perished and the charters of freedom were torn to shreds, the peasants collapsed into cowering submission. What hope of freedom was there when the King himself, recently so brave and gracious, was touring Kent and Essex with 40,000 soldiers?

'Villeins you were,' he told them, 'and villeins you are. In bondage you shall abide and not your old bondage but a worse!'

Yet the revolt was not in vain. When the savage punishment was over, there were not many lords who dared to tighten the old screws of feudalism. Times were changing, and although the peasants were never set free officially, they gained their freedom little by little. In time, most of them became landless labourers who worked for wages, poor and often wretched, but no longer serfs.

Richard II's moment of glory at Smithfield was his last. He had courage and ability, but as he grew up, he still showed the peevish temper and the extravagance of a spoilt child. Hating to be curbed by nobles or Parliament, he surrounded himself with elegant favourites and tried to rule like some grandiose monarch, until an opposition party led by his uncle, Thomas of Gloucester, brought him to his knees. A committee of nobles called the Lords Appellant took over the government and got rid of the King's friends by execution or banishment.

Richard, however, was no weakling. He bided his time and, a year later, he walked into the Council and asked his uncle how old he was:

'Your Highness is in your twenty-fourth year,' replied Gloucester.

'Then I am old enough to manage my own affairs,' said Richard coolly. 'I thank you for your services, my lords, but I need them no longer.'

For eight years, Richard governed well. He made peace with France, restored order in Ireland and treated everyone, including the Lollards, with tolerance and commonsense. His wife, Anne of Bohemia, seemed to have a good influence on him, but when she died in 1394, Richard married Isabella the daughter of the King of France with whom he made a peace treaty.

From this moment, Richard's character changed. Possibly his head was turned by the splendour of the French court; at all events, he suddenly struck like a vengeful tyrant at the nobles who had humiliated him eight years before.

Overawing Parliament by a force of archers drawn up in the Palace Yard at Westminster, Richard had his uncle murdered, his old opponents executed or banished and their estates confiscated, while he himself was granted taxes *for life* and a committee of his own friends to take the place of Parliament. Soon afterwards, he found an excuse to banish his own cousin Henry Bolingbroke, John of Gaunt's son.

In a delirium of triumph, Richard plunged into an orgy of tyranny and extravagance that made men wonder if he had become insane. In 1399, when his uncle, John of Gaunt, died, he seized his estates, the property of the exiled Bolingbroke, and with the money thus gained, he fitted out an expedition and sailed to Ireland.

In Richard's absence, Bolingbroke landed in Yorkshire, saying that he had merely come to claim his father's lands. His arrival was a signal to rebellion by all the King's opponents, who by this time included most of the nobles, the clergy, the merchants and every land-owner who feared for his family estates. Without strik-ing a blow, Henry Bolingbroke found himself presented with a kingdom, for when Richard landed from Ireland, his army deserted him and he fled in disguise to North Wales where he was captured and taken to London.

Stunned by his misfortune, this strange man, so tal-ented and so foolish, signed away his realm, declaring himself unfit to rule. Parliament then awarded the crown to his cousin Bolingbroke who thus became King Henry IV.

But there could be no safety with Richard alive, for he still had friends and he might again recover his brilliant abilities. Hustled from the Tower at night, he was im-prisoned in Pontefract Castle until 1400, when a re-bellion in his favour sealed his fate. His end was mysterious but although it was given out that he had starved himself to death, he was almost certainly mur-dered, for despite rumours that he was alive and at lib-erty, he was never seen again.

HENRY IV

A PLAIN, sturdy man and far more resolute than his elegant cousin, Henry IV had sufficient character to win respect; but as a usurper he had to tread warily to avoid offending the men who had set him on the throne. Thus, his whole reign was so beset with difficulties that he died worn out before he was fifty.

Having put down the rebellion of Richard's friends, Henry decided to subdue the Scots before they could assist France whose King was naturally enraged at the overthrow and murder of his son-in-law. But although he was a good soldier, Henry was unable to bring the Scots to battle. This failure was a blow to the King's reputation, all the more painful when the Earl of Northumberland and his son, Henry Percy, called Harry Hotspur defeated the Scots and captured many of their leaders.

Meanwhile, in Wales, Henry was faced by a national

rebellion. Owen Glendower, an educated, chivalrous gentleman, appealed to the King for justice against his English neighbour, Lord Grey of Ruthin, who had seized part of his estate. Henry unwilling to offend one of his nobles so early in his reign, sent Glendower packing and thereby roused a hornet's nest.

In 1400 Glendower sacked Ruthin and laid waste the countryside right up to the walls of Shrewsbury, but when Henry advanced with an army, the Welshmen retired to their mountains in scornful defiance. So many affairs required Henry's attention that he could do no more than leave his fourteen-year-old son, Prince Henry, to guard the border, and Owen soon became more troublesome than ever.

Henry's second attempt to crush the rebellion was no more successful. Hunger, heavy rain and incessant attacks by the agile Welsh troops forced the English army to retreat, and Owen Glendower, having captured Lord Grey, went rampaging into South Wales. There, at Bryn Glas, he defeated the English and made Sir Edmund Mortimer his prisoner.

Apart from a few castles, Glendower was now master of Wales and he lived in the style of an independent monarch, writing as an equal to the Kings of France and Scotland and making his plans for a Welsh parliament and university.

Meanwhile the Percies, having quarrelled with Henry over the ransoms of their Scottish prisoners, decided to throw in their lot with Owen Glendower. By this time the prisoner Mortimer was Glendower's friend and son-in-law.

Henry IV realized that this alliance, assisted by the French, could destroy him and he swiftly marched to Shrewsbury to tackle Hotspur before he could join forces with Glendower and Mortimer. In a hard-fought battle,

Henry and his son were victorious over the rebels; Hotspur was slain and his aged father surrendered later at York.

Glendower continued to defy the English King for several years but Prince Henry slowly ground him down and weakened his forces until the Welsh leader was reduced to wandering about the country, a defiant fugitive who refused to accept defeat or the pardon that was offered him by the Prince when he succeeded his father.

HENRY V

HENRY V had served a long apprenticeship to war
and, during his father's illness, he had practically ruled
the country. So, despite stories of wild adventures in his
youth, he came to the throne well-prepared for the role
that he meant to play.

One of the best-loved Kings in history, Henry looked
more like a priest than a warrior, with his grave expression and clear, unwavering gaze. He was noble-
minded and truly pious, although in the fashion of his
age, he could bear to watch a Lollard being burnt alive
and could allow civilians to die of starvation between the
walls of a beleaguered town and the lines of his besieging
army.

From Henry V's point of view, there seemed every

reason to re-open the war with France. The nobles loved fighting and the French had long been assisting the Welsh and the Scots; furthermore, the King of France was half-mad and his country was torn by bloodthirsty quarrels between the nobles. Lastly, for the sake of his conscience, Henry convinced himself that he had a claim to the French crown, although he had not the vestige of right to it.

In the summer of 1415 a well-equipped army of archers and men-at-arms landed in Normandy and laid seige to Harfleur. The fortress held out stoutly, and by the time it fell, autumn had set in and the usual camp-fever had reduced Henry's army to half its strength.

Not wishing to return home with so little in the way of success, the King decided to send the sick and wounded back by sea, while he marched to Calais with no more than 6,000 men. It was a rash venture, for the country-side had been stripped bare of provisions and the hungry soldiers had to trudge for seventeen days through continuous rain, existing as best they could on berries and nuts. The bridges over the Somme were down and during the days spent in finding a ford, the French were able to place a huge army astride the road to Calais.

There was no means of escape and Henry accepted battle at Agincourt. His famished men felt certain that they were doomed, but so great was their discipline and devotion to the King that each one resolved to die on the morrow giving as good an account of himself as possible. Henry V, however, had neither doubts nor fear. His air of confidence, his magnificent appearance in a surcoat resplendent with the leopards of England and the lilies of France and, above all, his ringing words filled his men with a fervour of courage that only death would subdue.

Henry drew up his little army, only four deep, behind

a row of sharpened stakes and presently advanced a short distance to provoke the French to attack across a newly sown wheat field which lay between two woods. Their front was narrow and as they pounded up the funnel-shaped gap, their ranks became so close packed that they scarcely had room to swing their weapons. Soon the heavily armoured foot soldiers could only flounder through churned-up mud and piles of corpses towards the English lines where the lightly clad archers, mostly stationed on either side of the men-at-arms and often skipping through the woods, shot them down with ease and then dropped their bows and came on with axes and swords. The second French attack advanced into disaster for, the more they pressed forward, the more impossible was it for them to fight at all.

In an absurdly short time the battle was over. Thousands of French knights perished and it was said that half the nobility of France died or were captured, whereas the English lost only a handful, so that even the King, still wearing the helmet and jewelled crown that had been dented in the fight, marvelled at the extent of his victory.

Agincourt brought no immediate gain, apart from the ransoms of so many distinguished captives, and the next three years were spent in hard campaigning, mostly devoted to sieges, that led to the conquest of Normandy and the capture of Rouen after a siege even more ghastly than the starving of Calais.

The road to Paris lay open and the French asked for peace. It was arranged that Henry should marry Catherine, the French King's daughter, should rule France during that poor monarch's lifetime and afterwards he and his heirs should succeed to the throne of France.

Henry married the Princess and after a visit to England they were back in France in 1422 when an attack of dysentery, the scourge of army camps, ended the King's life at the height of his fame and popularity. He was only thirty-three and he had begun to show far greater gifts than merely those of a successful soldier. Even a Frenchman said that he was 'valiant in arms, sage, great in justice who without respect of persons, did right for small and great'.

JAMES I OF SCOTLAND

THROUGHOUT the Hundred Years' War the Scots often assisted their French allies by making raids upon the north of England. In the year when Crecy was fought, Robert Bruce's son, David II, marched across the border but he was defeated and taken prisoner at Neville's Cross.

David was ransomed and when he died childless in 1371, the crown passed to Robert the Steward (or Stewart), son of Walter who had married Marjorie Bruce, daughter of the great King. During the reigns of Robert II and of his son Robert III, a lame and timid King, Scotland was an unhappy land torn by quarrels between its treacherous nobles and ravaged by the raids of the Highland clans upon the Lowlands and by perpetual war along the English border.

So black was the situation in 1406 that Robert III, in despair after the murder of his elder son, decided to send his other boy, James, to be brought up safely in France. Alas for his hopes, the ship with the Prince on board was captured by English pirates who handed over their captive to Henry IV.

This piece of fortune gave the English King too good a hold over the ancient enemy to let the young prisoner go home, even though his father had died and he was now James I of Scotland. For eighteen years, James lived in honourable captivity until Henry V permitted him to return to his native land with his beautiful English bride, Joan Beaufort.

James was a fine athlete, a musician and a poet who had had ample time during his captivity to consider how to govern his unruly kingdom. He speedily called a parliament and made it clear to the barons that he had come to put an end to their lawless ways. Private wars were forbidden, several nobles were executed for their past crimes and the Highland chiefs were kept in strict control.

For twelve years James ruled sternly and well, but many of his nobles longed for the days when they had been able to rob and plot to their hearts' content and some had not forgotten the punishment dealt out to them and their kinsmen.

In 1436 King James and the Queen went to spend Christmas in the monastery of the Black Friars at Perth where a royal party assembled for the season of festivities and tournaments. Unknown to James, the guests included several traitors who had sworn to take revenge for the King's stern measures.

In February, 1437, when the court was at dinner, the King's chamberlain left his seat and secretly removed the keys and bolts from the doors. Having laid planks across the moat to assist his fellow-traitors, he quietly returned to his place. The feasting and the dancing came to an end, the guests went to their bed-chambers and the King and Queen were about to retire to their own bower when James, feeling thirsty, sent his page to fetch some wine. In a corridor the boy ran into a band of armed men who had just entered the monastery with their leader, Sir Robert Graham, a fanatical enemy of the King. The page delayed the assassins by desperately defending himself with a dagger and the pewter wine-jug. The clatter of arms carried to the hall.

'Bolt the door!' ordered James, but the false chamberlain had removed the heavy bar and every weapon was gone.

'The vault, sire,' cried Catherine Douglas, one of the Queen's ladies. 'There is a vault under the floor!'

Snatching up a heavy pair of fire-tongs, James set furiously to work to prise up a floor-board and he was about to drop through the opening into the vault beneath when the traitors were heard approaching:

'Can you keep the door, if only for a minute?' cried the Queen who, with her women, was struggling to replace the board and to smooth its broken edges.

Catherine Douglas rushed to the door but it was hopeless for a woman to try to hold it against a band of murderous men. In despair, she thrust her bare arm through the iron loops where the bar had been. There was a push from outside but her arm held for a moment, then several men hurled their weight against the door and burst into the room as Catherine fell unconscious to the floor.

The conspirators looked round and the Queen faced them calmly, standing quite still so that her long skirt covered the tell-tale marks on the floor.

'The King? Where is the King?' they cried, and a ruffian held a knife to the Queen's throat.

'Leave her,' said Graham. 'We seek the King.'

At length, believing James to be in another part of the building, the conspirators clattered out and left the women alone. Presently, hearing a noise, they came back and found that James, thinking the danger past, was trying to clamber back into the room.

Two conspirators leapt down into the vault, but the King, as strong as a wrestler, had hurled them down, stunning the one and throttling the other, when, with a vengeful cry, Graham himself leapt down and buried his knife in the King's body.

The traitors fled and although the Queen and her people pursued them until all were taken and put to a horrible end, the harm to Scotland could not be undone The new King, James II, was a boy of six and the barons were free once more to pursue their lawless ways.

JOAN OF ARC

THE baby son of the victor of Agincourt was proclaimed Henry VI of England and soon afterwards, upon the death of Charles VI, he became King of France as well, according to the treaty that his father had made.

As Regent of France, it fell to the Duke of Bedford, a worthy brother of Henry V, to try to carry out the hopeless task of governing a country that had no wish to be ruled by the English.

Despite all his difficulties and the troubles made for him at home by his brother, Humphrey of Gloucester, Bedford won several victories over the French armies. By this time, they believed that the English were invincible and the listless behaviour of the Dauphin Charles did nothing to revive their spirits.

In 1428, when it seemed certain that Bedford would capture Orleans and snuff out all resistance, a miracle occurred.

A country girl named Jeanne d'Arc, or Joan of Arc, appeared at the Dauphin's court with a story that, while she was tending her father's sheep in the fields of Domrémy, heavenly voices told her that she alone could save France from the pitiless invader. Her air of absolute certainty gained her admittance, and the situation was so desperate that any ray of hope was welcome.

'The King of Heaven,' she cried to the Dauphin, 'bids me tell you that you shall be anointed and crowned in the Church of Rheims.'

Charles, smiling wearily at the maid's simplicity, agreed to allow her to attempt the impossible.

Clad in armour, Joan rode towards Orleans at the head of a company prepared to follow her in this harebrained scheme, and her glowing faith so inspired these soldiers that they drove the English from the strongpoint that dominated the city.

The siege was raised and soon afterwards Joan won a victory in the field at Patay. Within a year, as she had promised, Charles VII was crowned in Rheims Cathedral and the spirit of his countrymen was once more alive and strong.

Joan felt that her task was over but she stayed with the army because the soldiers' faith in her was so complete that they believed that she could lead them to absolute victory. Unfortunately they allowed her to decide military problems far beyond the girl's understanding. Naturally, she made mistakes and after failing in an attack on Paris, she was captured by the Burgundians, who handed her over to their English allies.

Tried for witchcraft by a court of churchmen presided over by the Bishop of Beauvais, Joan was pronounced guilty and, to the disgrace of the English, Burgundians and French alike, she was burned to death in the market-place at Rouen. As she died, clasping a rough cross and murmuring, 'Jesus,' an English soldier said: 'We are lost, for this maid was indeed a saint.'

It was several years before Joan's example brought the victory for which she died. The war swayed to and fro, with each side winning an occasional victory, but the French, fighting doggedly with Joan's name on their lips, slowly gained ground. Bedford, outnumbered and short of supplies, fought valiantly until his death in 1435, by which time the Burgundians had changed sides and he had rashly refused a peace offer that would have left Normandy and Aquitaine in English hands.

After this, the French won back their territories inch by inch and made such good use of cannons that, when the Hundred Years War ended in 1453, the English had lost almost everything, including Aquitaine, the great province that had been theirs since Henry II's marriage three hundred years before. Only Calais was left.

HENRY VI AND THE WARS OF THE ROSES

BEFORE the war ended Henry VI married Margaret of Anjou a fiery-tempered French Princess who naturally wanted peace with her native land. In this, she was supported by King Henry whose timid, courteous nature shrank from war.

Many of the nobles enjoyed fighting and they knew that, even in a hopeless war, there was plenty of excitement and pillage. So they opposed the Queen and her supporters (the Duke of Suffolk and his nephew Somerset) jeered at their plans for peace and blamed them for the continuous defeats in France.

So bitter was the feeling that King Henry sent Suffolk to Calais for safety, but his ship was intercepted by a vessel called the *Nicolas of the Tower* whose sailors greeted the Duke with shouts of, 'Welcome, traitor!' They dragged him on deck, hacked off his head and threw his body into the sea.

This murder of the King's adviser was followed by a rising of the turbulent men of Kent. Led by Jack Cade, they defeated the royal troops and entered London where they killed two ministers and fell to plundering the citizens. The Londoners indignantly set about the rebels, who retreated to their homes; Cade himself was killed and the rebellion fizzled out, but it showed the state of disorder into which the kingdom had fallen.

By this time, two hostile parties were arming their supporters. On one side were the Lancastrians, supporters of the King, whose badge was the red rose. On the other side were the Yorkists, wearers of the white rose, followers of Richard, Duke of York. He was Henry's cousin and heir to the throne for as long as the King had no children.

The nobles on both sides found it easy to recruit their forces from the soldiers home from France. These hardened campaigners were ready for any ugly work, whether it was on the battlefield or in some quiet village where a landowner could be terrorized into surrendering his rights to the lord whose badge they wore for pay.

In 1453 the pious King became mad and the Duke of York was made Protector of the realm, but the delight of his supporters changed to gloom when Queen Margaret, childless for nine years, gave birth to a healthy son and heir. King Henry recovered his wits as suddenly as they had flown from him, and the Queen had York dismissed from court:

'Let the Duke know that it is our purpose to make the King safe from his enemies,' she cried jubilantly, and with these threatening words, the Wars of the Roses began. It was only two years since the end of the Hundred Years' War.

York and his friends, including the Earl of Salisbury, his son, the Earl of Warwick, and the powerful Neville clan took up arms and marched towards London. At St. Albans, they found Somerset and the King holding the city with a strong force, but young Warwick burst through some houses and out into the streets. To cries of 'A Warwick! A Warwick!' he took the royal troops in the rear and won a resounding victory.

While Somerset's body lay on the steps of an inn, York and Warwick found the King in a cottage having an arrow wound in his neck dressed by a tanner's wife. They knelt to him and said that they had only come to

save him from his foes and to escort him safely to London.

When Henry became mad for the second time, York took control of the kingdom but Queen Margaret kept up such a relentless opposition that she was able to raise an army to scatter the Duke's forces. York fled to Ireland, while the dashing Warwick steered a small boat to Calais where he had been Governor for some time. With him were his father and Edward of March, York's eldest son, to whom he was now hero and protector.

The Queen straightway declared that the Yorkists had forfeited their lives and estates, so, with nothing to lose, they kept up the struggle and it was not long before they made another attack.

Warwick and young Edward of March crossed from Calais to Kent and, after a tumultuous welcome from the Londoners, who detested the Queen, they marched into the Midlands and defeated the royal army at Northampton. King Henry was captured and York claimed the crown. Hoping to prevent further bloodshed, Henry agreed to set aside his son's rights and to accept York as his successor.

This betrayal of her own child inflamed the Queen's bitterness. After adventurous wanderings in the Welsh mountains where a gang of robbers were said to have protected her and her little son, Queen Margaret reached Scotland and raised yet another army. The Duke of York marched north to meet this threat, and at Wakefield his troops were defeated and he himself was slain. The Earl of Salisbury was executed immediately after the battle. His head and York's, adorned by a paper crown, were set above the gate of the city of York.

Warwick advanced to avenge his father but Margaret's army beat him at the second battle of St. Albans and forced him to retreat to the Cotswolds where he joined Edward of March.

Margaret, who had recaptured her half-witted husband, had the game completely in her hands if she could have controlled her wild troops. But instead of capturing London, they preferred to straggle northwards, plundering the countryside as they went.

Warwick and Edward made a dash for the capital and, at a great meeting outside St. Paul's, the citizens agreed that King Henry was unfit to rule and that Edward of March, the Duke of York's son, should be King in his place.

After this bold stroke, the mighty Earl and the new monarch, Edward IV, set off to pursue the Lancastrian army, whose troops, disgusted at Henry's order forbidding plunder, were retreating in poor spirits.

In 1461 the armies met at Towton in Yorkshire where the Lancastrians were routed with the most terrible slaughter of any battle ever fought in England. Margaret and Henry fled to Scotland and Warwick proceeded to subdue the north with gruesome zest.

EDWARD IV

BY this time the Earl of Warwick was all-powerful, for Edward IV, handsome and indolent, seemed to have no thought for anything but banquets, tournaments and pretty ladies.

In order to make peace with the French, who had been helping Queen Margaret, Warwick arranged for Edward to marry a French princess. At the last moment, however, the King announced with an insolent smile that he was already secretly married to a beautiful lady named Elizabeth Woodville, widow of a Lancastrian.

Warwick swallowed his anger and made a great parade of escorting poor King Henry, recently captured in Lancashire, to the Tower. It was clear, however, that Edward IV had grown tired of being Warwick's puppet. He was about to shake off the great Earl and to destroy his power.

He promoted his wife's relatives, the Woodvilles, to positions of influence and having rid himself of Warwick's friends, he forbade his brother Clarence to marry the Earl's daughter Isabel. Clarence slipped away to Calais, married the girl and returned with his father-in-law to raise their supporters.

Taken by surprise, Edward smilingly surrendered to the Earl who now had two Kings in his power – Henry in the Tower and Edward in his camp. But Edward was too popular to be kept a prisoner for long. Warwick was obliged to set him free and thus to bring about his own downfall. Edward collected an army and so completely turned the tables that the Earl fled to France where Louis XI was already sheltering Queen Margaret and her son.

King Louis at once put forward an astonishing plan. Since Warwick and Edward IV were now enemies, he suggested that the Earl should change sides and put Henry VI back on his throne. It took patience to soothe the Queen's hatred of Warwick but, at last, the bargain was made, and in 1470 the Earl landed in Devonshire. The Queen was to follow and their supporters had already raised a rebellion to draw Edward north.

Finding that his army was riddled with treachery, Edward did not wait to fight. Instead, he fled to Flanders and Warwick the Kingmaker brought Henry VI out of the Tower and once again rode through the streets with the poor King whose sufferings had turned him into an imbecile.

But Warwick had forgotten his son-in-law, Clarence. That faithless nobleman had been quite content to see his brother overthrown if he himself should have the crown. But it was a different matter when the Lancastrian was back on the throne. He therefore made a secret promise to desert Warwick when the time was ripe.

At this, Edward IV decided to trust to luck and his own ability. He landed in Yorkshire, gathered an army and advanced to the Midlands where Warwick was confidently awaiting the arrival of Clarence. At the pre-arranged moment, Clarence threw away the red rose and led his troops to Edward's side.

Warwick still had a sizeable army, and although Queen Margaret had not arrived he attacked the Yorkists at Barnet on Easter Sunday, 1471. The battle was fought in a swirling mist and the Earl's troops were gaining the upper hand when the cry of, 'Treason! Treason!' was heard. The Earl of Oxford had arrived to aid Warwick, but in the mist his men, wearing his badge 'a star with rays', were mistaken for Yorkists whose badge was the rising sun. Attacked by their own allies, they fled. Panic followed; no commander could make himself obeyed and Warwick's army broke.

Later the mist cleared and the victorious Edward IV was surveying the field when his attention was drawn to a body stripped of its armour. It was Warwick the King-maker.

'There lies the last of the barons,' remarked Edward.

Queen Margaret and her son landed in England on that very day but they were defeated and captured at

Tewkesbury. The Prince was killed immediately and Margaret was sent to the Tower where, it was announced, King Henry died 'out of displeasure and melancholy'.

Having rid himself of all his opponents in battle or by execution, Edward IV had no rival for the rest of his life. In his cool, heartless way, he mastered the nobles and kept the respect of the middle-classes and of the common people. It was typical of him that when he took an army to France to punish Louis XI, he sensibly accepted a large sum of money instead of a battle and paid no heed to the indignation of his blood-thirsty nobles.

RICHARD III

EDWARD died suddenly in 1483, leaving two small sons. The elder boy became Edward V and, since he was only thirteen, it seemed right that he and his brother should be placed in the care of their uncle, Richard of Gloucester, who, as the late King's brother, was made Protector.

Gloucester immediately dismissed the unpopular Woodvilles, a move that frightened the Queen into taking sanctuary at Westminster, though she presently was persuaded into parting with her young son. He was sent to join his brother in the Tower where the young King had been placed 'for safety'.

With both Princes out of the way, Gloucester ordered the execution or imprisonment of all who seemed likely to oppose him. Then he claimed the throne on the grounds that Edward IV's marriage was illegal and he had himself crowned Richard III just two weeks after the date fixed for his nephew's coronation.

The two Princes were never seen in public again. Rumours of their death went about, and twenty years later Sir James Tyrrel confessed that he and two servants had been ordered to kill the boys. This story seemed to be confirmed when two small skeletons were found in the Tower in 1674.

Richard III, nicknamed 'Crookback' by his enemies, was a first-rate general, brave, charming and absolutely loyal to his brother, Edward IV, who liked and trusted him. Could such a man have murdered his own nephews? It is certain that he had grown up in the treacherous, violent years of the Wars of the Roses and he knew all too well that the way to win power was to strike suddenly without scruple or pity.

At all events, he was now King with every rival dead and nothing to fear. There was, however, just one young man left alive who could claim the throne, and luckily for him he was out of Richard's reach.

This young man, the last hope of the Lancastrians, had been sent abroad for safety and was now living in Brittany. He was Henry Tudor, Earl of Richmond, and his mother was a descendant of John of Gaunt and therefore of Edward III.

To avoid Richard III's agents, Henry went to France where he found sufficient help to decide to risk his life to win a crown.

In August 1485 he landed at Milford Haven in the land of his Welsh grandfather, Owen Tudor. Numbers of Welshmen joined him and although he had only 5,000 men by the time he reached Shrewsbury, he had good reason to believe that some of Richard III's so-called supporters would hold off and others, notably Lord Stanley and his brother, Sir William Stanley, would assist him.

The King met his rival at Bosworth Field in Leicestershire, and at the critical moment Stanley changed sides. Richard III was no coward and he fought with furious courage to the end. The crown that he wore in the battle was picked up from beneath a bush and placed on the head of the victor, who thus became Henry VII, first of the Tudor monarchs.

WILLIAM CAXTON THE PRINTER

EVEN in the most violent periods of our history, men continued to write poetry, to build wonderful churches, to found schools and universities and to manage the affairs of their towns and guilds. Among these writers, scholars and industrious citizens was a sober merchant whose achievements outshone the deeds of almost all the kings and nobles. He was William Caxton.

Born in Kent when Henry VI was a child, Caxton served as a boy-apprentice to a mercer or cloth-merchant in the city of London. When he was a young man, he went to Bruges, one of the cloth cities of Flanders, and set up in business for himself. He travelled, he grew rich and he rose to be the chief English merchant in the Low Countries, and like many rich men, he was able to enjoy an expensive hobby. His greatest pride was his collection of books – rare and beautiful books, written by hand so carefully and so slowly that a man with a dozen books possessed a proud library; but Caxton wanted more than this and not merely for himself.

He heard that Master Gutenberg in Germany had invented a way of *printing* books faster than a man could write and he went to Cologne to see this marvellous invention called a printing *press*, because it pressed sheets of paper on to wooden letters that had been fitted into a frame.

Caxton and his assistant built a press of their own, and in the reign of Edward IV they came to England and set up the press in a house close to Westminster Abbey. The wool merchant devoted the rest of his life to printing stories, poems and ballads and it was his work and the work of other printers that marked the end of the Middle Ages and the beginning of a new age.

Index

THE STORY OF MAUDE REED *by Norah Lofts*   25p

552 52010 1   Carousel Fiction

Her grandfather was only a wool merchant and his house was not considered suitable for a young girl of noble blood. Maude was now old enough to be taught the accomplishments of a lady; sewing, music and the art of graceful behaviour. But this was the Fifteenth Century, and her school was to be an old dark castle.

HAVELOK THE WARRIOR *by Ian Serraillier*   20p

552 52007 1   Carousel Fiction

These are the days when evil men conspire to overthrow the monarchy, greedy for the power and wealth of wearing the crown and ruling the land. The King of Denmark is dead, his son Havelok forced to flee the murderous attempts of Earl Godard by escaping to the shores of England. He grows up to be a great warrior, to recover his kingdom.

EVERYDAY LIFE IN PREHISTORIC TIMES
by Marjorie and C.H.B. Quennell   each 25p

552 54005 6   Carousel Non-Fiction
552 54006 4

This series presents a picture in words of how our forefathers lived in their prehistoric world, moving out of their caves into the earliest settlements; discovering metals; making fires; building and constructing the first organized villages. The EVERDAY LIFE series follows them, detailing their development into civilization as we know it.